JOHN KILLICK was a teach  er
since his early years. For ⟩n
communication with pec el-
low and as a freelance.] ks
on the subject, most recently *The Story of* __ th,
2017), *Poetry and Dementia* (Jessica Kingsley Publications,
2017) and *Dementia Positive* (Luath, 2013).

Amongst his general literary works are *Writing for Self-Discovery* (Element Books and Barnes & Noble Books, 1998) and *Writing Your Self* (Continuum, 2003) – both co-edited with Myra Schneider. He has also been a small press publisher (Littlewood, 1982–91). His books of poetry include *Windhorse* (Rockingham, 1996) and *Inexplicable Occasions* (Fisherrow, 2017).

As an only child himself, he has attempted to come to terms with his situation throughout his life.

Onlyness

Exploring the Predicament of the Only Child

JOHN KILLICK

Luath Press Limited

EDINBURGH

www.luath.co.uk

First published 2019

ISBN: 978-1-910745-48-9

The paper used in this book is recyclable. It is made from low chlorine pulps produced in a low energy, low emission manner from renewable forests.

Printed and bound by iPrint Global Ltd., Ely

Typeset in 11 point Sabon by Lapiz

Dedicated to the memory of my parents
who endured my early struggles

Contents

Introduction

The starting point for this book was reflections on being an only child, and an attempt to trace the development of social awareness and participation whilst retaining one's essential solitariness. It was never my intention to write an autobiography, but to draw on events from my life to make the struggle come alive. I have read, in any case, too many life stories which mingle the prosaic and the memorable in an unhappy melange. As well as the mundane, I have rigorously excluded references to friends and family amongst the living, preferring to concentrate on the development of roles and relationships in the wider world.

I have from an early age kept journals, and I have raided these for evocations of specific people and events. I have also drawn on a number of my published essays and articles. About a dozen pieces have been specially written to fill gaps in the record.

A further dozen pieces have been written to provide signposts on the journey. They have been composed in a more objective manner, but they reflect my opinions. Most of the pieces vary between narrative and poetic evocation, with a handful in the form of dialogues. I have kept them all short, in the interests of immediacy. A perhaps controversial aspect of the style employed is the predominance of the present tense. This has its drawbacks and I am aware it can cause irritation, but I believe the immediate involvement of the reader is worth the risk.

The book generally follows the chronology of my life, but where a theme is indicated I have not hesitated to break the pattern, believing that a piece can contribute more when grouped with its fellows than strictly adhering to a time-scale.

I have included a number of dreams. In his autobiography, Edwin Muir stressed dreams as a significant part of each individual's life, and I agree with that judgement. By stressing the link between conscious and unconscious experience I think they can illuminate any attempt to portray the psyche.

All the above refers to Part Two of the book. When I had finished assembling the pieces which constitute the major part of the text, I was very aware of the highly subjective nature of the account, and felt it should be balanced by a short essay prefacing it giving a wider series of views of a subject which has preoccupied writers and researchers over recent decades. This is by no means comprehensive, but offers a guide to some of the main viewpoints to have emerged.

I must acknowledge the following sources for earlier versions of some of these pieces in Part Two:

The London Magazine, Poetry Review, The Reader, The Times Educational Supplement, Writing in Education, The Journal of Dementia Care and the books *Dementia Diary* (Hawker) and *Writing Your Self* (Continuum).

PART ONE:

An Objective View

Suppose you woke up one day and couldn't remember whether you were an only child or not – how, apart from asking others, might you find out? Jill Pitkeathley and David Emerson, in their book *Only Child: How to Survive Being One*[1], suggest placing yourself in a group situation and asking yourself the following questions – who is:

> *the most responsible person in the group?*
> *the most organised?*
> *the most serious?*
> *the one who is rarely late?*
> *the one who doesn't like arguments?*
> *the self-possessed one?*

The chances are that the one who is all these things will be the only child.

It's not infallible but it's pretty reliable as a test.

Of course nobody chooses onlyness; it is a condition which, for good or ill, you are stuck with. And just as those with siblings know nothing different, 'onlies' cannot experience what it is like to feel and act as a member of the other family subdivision.

Though that is not strictly true. In considering the nature of onlyness one has to consider that we are not dealing with one concept fits all. As with so many subjects, the simple generalisations keep needing to be unpicked once you get into the details.

Take the definition, for instance. We are not just dealing with the straightforward 'two parents, one offspring' set-up. We need to encompass the role of the eldest child before other children come along, the youngest after the others may even have flown the nest, the survivor after siblings have perished; all these can experience periods of onlyness. Then there are those who may be singled out for special treatment by the parents and treated with a degree of onlyness, like the disabled child with abled companions, the gender-favoured child, and the star performer amongst mediocre companions. And in a society where divorce and remarriage are commonplace, there is the adjustment an only may have to make when finding him or herself suddenly with brothers and sisters. Then there is the experience of an only being born into a one-parent family: the dynamic here could be quite different. Any of these occurrences may break the mould, or at the least call for a dramatic adjustment to be made. There is a common observation that if you have spent seven years as an only at any period of your life you count as one.

Nevertheless, there are characteristics of onlyness which can be identified, however much circumstances may later involve their modification. Carl E Pickhardt is a medical doctor who has done a great deal of counselling of families with onlies, and onlies themselves. His book *The Future of Your Only Child*[2] is the fruit of this work. He has provided a stimulating list of what he has identified as the common characteristics of only children, which I will label 'The Ten C's':

> *Compliant – the tendency to fit in with social norms*
> *Concerned – seeking adult approval for behaviour*
> *Centre – wanting to be the focus of attention*
> *Caution – the reluctance to take risks*
> *Conservative – resistance to change*
> *Commitment – adherence to a set of values*
> *Control – the tendency to manage relationships*
> *Content – being comfortable with solitude*
> *Critical – applying high standards to self and others*
> *Conflict-avoidance – dislike of confrontation*

Taken together, these form a useful pattern of an only's attitude to life.

Pickhardt has also come up with the term for onlies as 'People of the "Should"'. By this he means that they have an overarching sense of right behaviour, which is one of their strongest characteristics. He notes that the word 'should' occurs frequently in their sentences, and they lean upon conscience to determine their moral stances.

In popular culture, what do The Exorcist, Batman and Superman have in common? Yes, they were all conceived of and act as onlies.

What do all these people have in common: Leonardo da Vinci, Isaac Newton, Mahatma Gandhi, Frank Sinatra, Elvis Presley, Elton John, John Lennon, Iris Murdoch, Jean Paul Sartre? Yes, they were/are all onlies. No doubt a rival respectable list could be compiled of those who were/are not. Nevertheless, it is impressive.

Ann Laybourn in her 1990 book *Children and Society*[3] found that:

> Despite the fact that they tended to come from less advantaged backgrounds only children performed similarly or slightly better than those from a two-child background on behavioural and educational measures.

This ties in with Pickhardt's emphasis on ambition as a key characteristic. He believes that the only child, having only the parents to measure up to, assumes equal standing with them, adopts equal performance standards, and strives after equal competencies as well. The role of parents in setting even higher standards for their sole offspring is a further crucial factor. Pickhardt quotes a mother as saying:

> Many parents have vicarious dreams for their children, but parents of only children have epic visions.

and an advice columnist of committing herself to the following revealing statement in a letter to her daughter:

> I am still your mother and it is MY responsibility to see that nothing spoils my masterpiece.

It is hardly surprising, then, to find an only child such as Jean Paul Sartre (in his autobiography *Words*[4]) rising to the challenge:

> It is not enough for my character to be good. It must also be prophetic.

Of all the apologists for onlyness, Pickhardt is by far the most specific. There are few aspects he does not cover, and his text is full of thought-provoking observations. Take this one, for example:

The critical effect of having no siblings is <u>not</u> that the only child is deprived of a big happy family and suffers from missing the good feeling companionship with other children at home. The critical effect is that the only child is deprived of a big <u>unhappy</u> family, not all the time, but enough of the time so that the ups and downs of intermittent unhappiness, with siblings particularly, are not experienced as a normal part of family life.

If academia is one area in which only children are seen to at least hold their own, creativity is one where they have the opportunity to excel. Having the time and space to explore themselves and develop their talents may prove a real advantage, and can lead to setting ambitious standards. This may stem from the opportunities for daydreaming that aloneness provides; many only children speak of populating their childhoods with fantasy creatures, people and even whole worlds.

'The Handless Maiden' is a Grimm's Fairytale in which the girl's father, tempted by the devil, and driven wholly by materialist motives, cuts off his daughter's hands. She leaves home and wanders in the forest. A king finds her eating the fruit from a tree in his orchard. He doesn't penalise her because he falls in love with her; he gifts her silver replacement hands. She bears his child, but, just as at home, when she was handless everything was done for her, at court she lives a life of enforced idleness. Again she escapes to the forest, this time with her baby. She is bathing the child in the river when her silver hands get wet. Her actual hands are restored to her.

This has been interpreted as a story about the only child exercising creativity in adversity. Jungian analysts have seen it as an archetypal fable of the Journey of the Self. The hands symbolise her taking hold of her life, and the restoration of them to her in place of the false ones means she has been enabled through her actions to connect inner and outer worlds.

Of course many writers of prose and poetry have reflected onlyness in their work. This is particularly true of autobiographers. It is interesting to compare two of the latter who have both boldly entitled the story of their lives *An Only Child* and *The Only Child* respectively. These two writers are Frank O'Connor[5] and James Kirkup[6]. The two books have much in common. They both chronicle working-class childhoods, the one in Cork in Ireland and the other South Shields on Tyneside. They both cover limited periods of time: the first 18 years and the second six years. They are both strong on relationships and descriptions of environments. O'Connor is stronger on people portraits, and Kirkup on physical evocations. And the most extraordinary of their similarities is, despite their choice of titles, how little either of them has to say overtly on the only child situation.

O'Connor has a single sentence which reveals his awareness of the consequences for him of being an only: 'I had already become a classic example of the Mother's Boy'. But the reader cannot but be struck by the amount of space given over to the mother in his narrative: 30 pages are devoted to evoking her, and 20 of these constitute an account of her life before the author's birth; this is in a book of 175 pages where her presence looms large elsewhere too.

Kirkup is notable too for his lack of reflection on his status. One of the few passages stands out for its distinctiveness in this regard:

> I was a lonely child, though I was not conscious of loneliness, in fact I preferred being on my own. At the same time I was torn by the desire to be with people, to be part of a circle. I loved the idea of 'being together' with Whitmanesque intensity. Yet after 'being together' with my cousins for a while I longed to be alone. I couldn't understand myself. It was the beginning of a conflict that was to distress me for many years.

These books are outstanding examples of where the theme is underlying the narrative – we understand onlyness only by implication throughout.

Bernice Sorensen[7], a psychotherapist, in her book *Only Child Experience and Adulthood* characterises only child life patterns as follows:

> The sense of being special, but alone and sometimes lonely. The feeling of disconnection from their own and other childishness. The enjoyment of times alone in their intra-psychic worlds, whilst experiencing alienation from the inter-personal or social world.

Psychoanalysis has a good deal to say about birth order. It was of little interest to Freud, but Alfred Adler[8] saw the only child as essentially a spoilt child:

> An only child is pampered by his mother. She is afraid of losing him and wants to keep him under her attention. He develops what is called 'a mother complex', he is tied to his mother's

> apron strings and wishes to push his father out
> of the family picture.

Some psychologists believe that the most significant characteristic which separates onlies from others in the birth order is that between introversion and extroversion. Carl Jung was the thinker most associated with this theory. He claimed that other-directed persons were interested in the external world, and introverts were preoccupied with their own thoughts and feelings. Some commentators have seen onlies fitting naturally into the latter category, but others have identified a conflict between the two tendencies as being central to their lifestyles.

There is no doubt that over the years only children have had a bad press. The American psychologist Granville Stanley Hall in the book *Of Peculiar and Exceptional Children* published in 1896[9] saw them as misfits who were incapable of adjustment. He even stated:

> Being an only child is a disease in itself.

Judith Blake, in her book *Family Size and Achievement*[10] uses the following pejorative terms:

> ...over-privileged, asocial, royally autonomous,
> self-centred, aloof, overly intellectual.

In rejecting the commonly held prejudices, Sorensen appears to throw out every possible effect of birth-order:

> People articulate that only children are spoiled,
> they're aggressive, they're bossy, they're lonely,
> they're maladjusted. There are hundreds and
> hundreds of research studies that only children
> are no different from their peers.

Despite the academic research which Sorensen cites, there are, of course, hundreds and hundreds of personal accounts by onlies of being bullied, castigated and discriminated against because of their perceived characteristics. Adriean Mancillas[11], an American educational psychologist, takes the opposite view from Sorensen, and demonstrates in her work how recalcitrant such mindsets are to amelioration. She states:

> Even when people consider that most only children may indeed possess positive characteristics, the tendency exists for them to dismiss such strengths as emanating from an environment that is overly indulgent.

and attributes their stubbornness to change as a lack of will on the part of society to address the issues:

> It's not like racial stereotyping, which you can demonstrate is really dangerous for people, so we've had to address it. With only children, there's no impetus to weaken the belief.

The widest range of texts is by 'experts' giving advice to parents. In *The Seven Common Sins of Parenting an Only Child: a Guide for Parents, Kids and Families* Carolyn White[12] (editor of a magazine titled *Only Child*) confidently proposes the following:

> Overindulgence
> Overprotection
> Failure to Discipline
> Overcompensation
> Seeking Perfection
> Treating Your Child Like an Adult
> Overpraising

Nachman and Thompson[13] in their *You and Your Only Child: the Joys, Myths and Challenges of Raising an Only Child* also offer a list, but shorter and subtler:

(1) Recognise the intensity of your relationship with your child
(2) Recognise that all your expectations, fantasies, hopes and dreams are involved
(3) Distinguish between the grown-ups' world and the child's world

It was surprising to find Carolyn White identifying 'kids' as intended readers of her book. These would necessarily be older onlies. What is on offer for younger children? Outstanding for the quality of its writing is Anne Fine's *The Only Child Club*[14]. Ryan is fed up being an only so he decides to start an Only Child Club. He is acutely conscious that he is missing out on the experiences of some of his classmates so he invites two onlies to join. They spend a few days together quarrelling and unsuccessfully model-making. The limited experience of what it might be like to have siblings cures all three of their envy, and they are happy to resume their previous roles as friends. The story is told wittily and un-dogmatically.

A much racier and more provocative book for the youngest age group is *Because I am the Only Child,* verses by Loretta Campbell and illustrations by Grant H Alwood[15]. Here is a sample:

This is my Mam and Dad,
and I'm their only son.
You don't see any siblings
because I'm the only one...

When it's time for dessert
I get to eat the last slice.
And when I need Dad's attention
I don't have to ask twice.

To imagine the illustrations, think Dr Seuss. It's fairly obvious stuff and the child would certainly get the message.

What about the statistics of onlyness: is it a recent phenomenon, or has it always been with us? It is largely a 20th century invention, because of a number of factors, perhaps the most significant being family planning, economic necessity and late marriages. The UK has one of the highest incidences in Western Europe with 47 per cent of homes with children consisting of one-child families and rising, resulting in some commentators hailing it as the lifestyle choice of couples in future decades.

The one-child policy in China, sometimes referred to as the 'Little Emperor Syndrome', was brought in by Deng Xiaoping in 1979. It had two basic aims: to reduce a population getting out of control, and to create a nation of high achievers, based on the theory that each additional child in a family dilutes resources. It has undoubtedly been very successful in both aims. There has been considerable pressure to relax the rule, both from parents and the children themselves. After decades, this has now occurred, but too late to prevent a serious imbalance in the country with far too few young people having to support a large ageing population. Currently 90 per cent of children in the country are onlies, totalling one hundred million. Feng Xiaotian[16], a sociologist from Nanjing University, has emphasised the positive nature of the experiment in the following judgement:

> Only children get greater compensation from
> social behaviour – this means teenage only chil-
> dren learn even more, are even better-tempered
> and become even more tolerant.

A fundamental question I have ducked so far, which needs
to be posed, is: 'How close is onlyness to loneliness?' No
doubt some would answer 'very close'. They have gone
through their lives feeling the lack of an intimate companion acutely, and it may have affected their choice of a life
partner, and the subsequent success or failure of that relationship. Expectations may be just too high. And whether
that choice is of another only, or of someone with wide sibling experience, can be expected to play a part. Then there
is parenthood itself. Onlies as mothers or fathers are likely
to replicate their own experiences in bringing up a child, or
to strive to make things as different as possible for their offspring. But they may fail to understand, if they bring more
than one infant into the world, what the communal experience is like and make a series of serious mistakes. Pitkeathley
and Emerson make the connection between onlyness and
loneliness in this way:

> From the only children to whom we have talked,
> it is clear there is a set of pressures felt to a great-
> er or lesser extent by all of them. Having had
> to be everything to their parents, they have had
> to carry a heavy burden of responsibility, expec-
> tation and blame. Because they lacked experi-
> ence of what they called 'rough and tumble' of
> emotional life, they had difficulties with their
> self image and were inclined to be emotionally
> immature behind a confident, grown up exterior.

> Most of them felt that, in the end, the only child
> is always alone.

Their book, also quoted at the outset of this little essay, is the one to read for a spectrum of views on onlyness by onlies. *One and Only: The Freedom of Having an Only Child and the Joy of Being One* by Lauren S Sandler[17] is probably the best proselytising text. It may be confusing having to come to terms with such contradictory materials, but a wide spectrum constitutes a realistic basis for exploring the parameters of the subject. But then one comes up against a quote like the following from the American novelist Thomas Wolfe, to which the only response is silence:

> Loneliness... is and always has been the central
> and inevitable experience of every man.[19]

That may be the last word on loneliness, but from me the last word must be about onlyness. In researching the subject, I kept encountering the idea of intensity. If there is one thing which all commentators agree on it is the unavoidably deep emotional experience of the triadic relationship. Whether it is partial and time-limited or total, whether it is holistic or dysfunctional, it has the capacity to spread its tentacles throughout the only's life, shaping his/her decision-making and achievements. Prophecy Coles[18] sums up the situation thus:

> I am aware there is a qualitative difference in
> the feel of the inner world of only children com-
> pared to those who have siblings.

References

1)   Pitkeathley J, Emerson D (1994) *Only Child: How to Survive Being One.* London: Souvenir Press.

2)   Pickhardt C E (2008) *The Future of Your Only Child.* New York: Palgrave Macmillan.

3)   Laybourn A (1990) *Children and Society.*

4)   Sartre J P (1964) *Words.* London: Hamish Hamilton.

5)   O'Connor F (1961) *An Only Child* London: Macmillan.

6)   Kirkup J (1957) *The Only Child: An Autobiography of Infancy. Collins.*

7)   Sorensen B (2008) *Only Child Experience and Adulthood.* Basingstoke: Palgrave Macmillan.

8)   Adler A (1962) *What Life Should Mean to You.* London: Unwin.

9)   Hall G S (1896) in Bohannon E H *Of Peculiar and Exceptional Children.*

10) Blake J (1992) *Family Size and Achievement.* Berkeley: University of California Press.

11) Mancillas A (2006) 'Challenging the Stereotypes about Only Children: A Review of the Literature and Implications for Practice', *Journal of Counseling and Development* (Summer 2006).

12) White C (2004) *The Seven Common Sins of Parenting An Only Child: A Guide For Parents, Kids and Families.* San Francisco: Jossey-Bass.

13) Nachman P, Thompson A (1997) *You and Your Only Child: The Joys, Myths and Challenges of Raising an Only Child* New York: Harper Collins.

14) Fine A (2014) *The Only Child Club.* London: Walker Books.

15) Campbell L, Almond G H *Because I am the Only Child*. Amazon: CreatesSpace Independent Publishing Platform.

16) Xiaotian F (2003) *Only Children: Their Families, Education and Future.*

17) Sandler L (2013) *One And Only: The Freedom of Having an Only Child, and the Joy of Being One.* New York: Simon and Schuster.

18) Coles P (2003) *The Importance of Sibling Relationships in Psychoanalysis*. London: Karnak.

19) Wolfe T (2011) *You Can't Go Home Again*. New York: Scribner.

PART TWO:

A Personal Story

The Challenge of Childhood

Onlyness begins in childhood.

And there for some it ends: or rather, they so throw themselves into activity, into community, that they hardly have time to take breath, let alone consider the implications of their situation.

Yet others, whilst attempting to integrate, are constantly aware of their solitary status, its drawbacks and its privileges.

All have the same origins, however: a sense of uniqueness, and an essential fragility of experience, which underlies everything they do, whether they are aware of it or not.

They don't have to fight for their inheritance, but they always feel the need to justify their existence, in their own as well as others' eyes.

The story of their beginning is also the story of their end. Onlyness provides the opportunity for the appreciation of life as a perfect circle.

Only

In my childhood world I was the little god. Everywhere I trod was open, unobstructed. My pets, my toys, my thoughts need never be shared. Parents and friends attended.

Life was at one remove: everything outside myself left me unmoved. Mooning in windows, I stayed secure behind plate-glass. I could have waved a hand, like royalty, as they passed.

When I went for walks I chose the sand-dunes: skylarks piped and spun in the sun overhead, the crass marram-grass bit into my bare legs – I maintained my pride.

But all things must pass: now the toys are lost, the glass is smashed, the dunes developed. Only my mind still keeps a stance apart to interpret the heart.

One Morning

I am lying on my parents' bed and the bedclothes almost completely envelop me. The pleasure rolls over me in waves of sheer womb-enclosed warmth. There is no-one else in the room. My mother and father are already up. My father is dressed and breakfasted, my mother is still in her nightie and dressing-gown, and is with him in the kitchen where she has been cooking his breakfast; his departure for work is one of the major events in the day. My black-and-white-spotted mongrel Timmy has gone out for an exploration of the yard and garden; this is a modest semi-detached house in a suburb of a dormitory town. There are muddy paw-prints on the eiderdown where Timmy got into this room yesterday, much to my mother's fury, and left a trail of destructive enthusiasm over the furniture.

My mother is house-proud. The bedroom is usually spotless. Surfaces shine; the dressing table mirror is blemish-free. All around the room are reminders of my mother's femininity and family ties: the wallpapers are exquisitely decorative; there are photographs of her parents, her wedding-group, and some of myself. Even at six I find the claustrophobia of this room palpable, and yet part of myself gladly submits to it, like I am at present burrowing into the bedclothes. I can smell the sweet perfume her body exudes. I am lying in the hollow she has mapped out on the mattress. If I wait here long enough she may be persuaded to bring me breakfast in bed and to join me for a lie-in afterwards.

I hear the sound of the car on the drive. My father is leaving for the station. He has not called up to say goodbye – he probably thinks I am asleep.

Suddenly my mother bursts into the room. Tears are coursing down her cheeks. Without a word she throws herself down on the bed beside me and clasps me in her arms. She is crying so uncontrollably that the tears transfer from her cheeks onto mine, forming a rivulet that wets my pyjamas.

All she can say is 'John, John, John!' Then, 'Timmy! – your father!'

I leap from the bed, run through the corridor, down the stairs, into the kitchen and out of the backdoor. My father is walking slowly up the drive towards me holding in his outstretched arms the body of my dog.

The Brother

Why is my mother so happy? Why is she so large? Why does she go into even more smiley huddles with my father than usual? Why is she even more indulgent to me than usual? Why is he so indulgent to me? It seems I can ask for anything I want. A pedal-car? It is produced. More carriages for my trainset? They miraculously appear. This is great. This is holiday mood lasting throughout the year.

Then my mother disappears. She has gone away for a few days, I am told. She will return with something new, something very special. Will it be for me? Not another treat? This is almost too much…

She returns with The Brother: this is David, I am told. He is tiny, noisy and smelly. He is doted upon. I decide to tolerate him for the time being, for the sake of family peace.

Then a drama unfolds. We are suddenly surrounded by strangers with worried frowns on their faces. My mother, this time taking The Brother with her, is gone again.

When she returns she is alone. She cannot stop crying. But these are not ordinary tears – she is howling, like an animal in pain. She appears inconsolable. My father stands there helplessly wringing his hands. Neither of them has any time for me. I stay in my bedroom telling stories to my teddy bear.

*****

Months later I am crowing, cock on midden. Now, for me, it is what has not changed that has made all the difference.

A Grandfather

I sit on his knee in the big leather armchair with the brass plaque on the side commemorating his years of service to the state. I am there to hear the fantastic tales he makes up or reads from 'Wee McGregor' by JJ Bell. I adore them and him: his wonderful lined face, blue eyes that twinkle, hair sprouting from everywhere, a browning moustache that looks as if it has been used as a strainer for various liquids. Although we live in Lancashire, he is a Scotsman from Bo'ness and has been an excise man inspecting distilleries. He has a huge pocket-watch on a gold chain (given him to mark his retirement); he takes it out and looks at it solemnly when he thinks my mealtime or bedtime might be approaching.

He takes his responsibilities as a storyteller seriously. Waiting for the next twist of the plot or the next burst of Glaswegian dialect is a thrill. Then there is the smell of Rennies he takes for his indigestion; sometimes he gives me one which I pretend to enjoy as a sweet. All the time Granny tut-tuts around us – she doesn't approve of small boys being indulged in any way.

Increasingly Grandad takes little turns in which he temporarily loses consciousness. One day I shake him and run for Granny and the sal volatile as usual. But neither she, nor my mother, nor the doctor, can wake him. He has died in the middle of telling me a story.

The Big House

We have moved to a much larger Victorian house in a more prosperous suburb. The entrance is guarded by a pair of stone lions. You have to climb a pair of stone steps to reach them. I run my hands over their manes and tails and the ruffs round their necks. They, and the stone border running down to a wide sweep of gravel, are painted cream. Huge copper beeches tower over the driveway.

Walking in the house is a matter of entering room after room; high ceilings and seemingly endless floors. There is a great expanse of walls, with few pictures. You are conscious of height, width, solidity. The ceilings have stucco friezes and large chandeliers hang from the centre. These rooms are places where you might breathe, feel your identity grow, inhabit the space. But at the same time, they inhibit, cow, make you feel insignificant. Even with people in them the rooms seem empty. I don't know this but I will always see them through the eyes of a child, never as an adult.

The large windows are the most significant features of the rooms. Outside lies the world: people and traffic passing. My face is pressed to the glass. I see them, they don't see me. I long to be part of what is out there, of what always seems to be in movement, in contrast to the stasis I inhabit. I cannot be myself in here, so how can I possibly be myself elsewhere? I am fearful, and the fear is that wherever I am I won't be able to cope. I don't know my own size – am I large or small? I have nothing and nobody to measure up to. I am the only Only in the world.

The Wave

Of the people in the house, my grandmother and grandfather are now dead. My father is increasingly away at work. There is only my mother to engage in relationship. She has an overwhelming need to draw her consolations from me. She is a woman of talent and potential. Her marriage cramps her, so she increasingly pours her unused feelings in my direction. She is so beautiful: a portrait should have been painted of her. Her smile draws me to her: she so attracts me that I must be in her presence; temporarily she blots out the house's (and the world's) alien expanses.

When I pull myself away there is reproof in her eyes. Then she turns upon my father the full force of her radiance. She must be at the centre of everything for both of us. She has far more love than the two of us can ever absorb. It is like a liquid flowing over us.

No wonder I play in attics games which involve miniature environments which can be comprehended and controlled. If the tidal wave laps here and withdraws, there is some small chance my life may be saved.

The Gate

A big house needs a big drive and this house has one. A big drive needs a big gate and this house has one of those too, though it is not quite what you might expect. The house is Victorian but the gate is a low-slung wooden structure, green-painted and '30s in style. The lower two-thirds are solid and the top-third is open with a criss-cross pattern but with a top bar that is substantial, good for leaning on. At first, though, I am not tall enough to reach the top, so I hang on the lower shelf and peer through the slats. There is just room for my feet to fit under the gate, so I can look down and see my toes peeping out of my sandals. In summer, I can also see the rolls of dust that collect at the foot of the pillars inside and outside the gate and, amongst the assorted debris, there are always little piles of hedge-clippings which my father has failed to collect, and which blew and lodged there. Sometimes the gate is so hot that I can hardly put my hand on it.

The gate is the border of our property and also marks the margin of my private world. I spend much of my time with my nose pressed to the many windows in the house, but when the weather permits, I trot down to the gate to take a closer look. Sometimes people in the street speak to me, and I attempt a shy conversation, but mostly they ignore me. They are too concerned with crossing the road safely or catching a bus and do not even notice my presence. Nevertheless, my parents disapprove of my behaviour (the word 'common' is used) and keep calling me away to reprimand me, or send me on errands which, I suspect, are made up for the purpose of distracting me.

The Gate (later)

Over the course of time, the gate rots and begins to fall apart. Instead of mending it, my parents decide to await the inevitable. I am bigger and heavier by this time and am warned to treat the gate with consideration: in other words, no more climbing on it. All my care cannot save my beloved gate from swift collapse. One day it is carted away and a gap exists where it had been, much wider, it seems to me, than that which the gate had filled. I am horrified by this degree of exposure. I can see everything I want to but there is nothing to offer me even partial protection. Dogs wander in off the street and mess on the lawns and borders. People who stand on the corner outside now seem to spend their time peering into the garden and at the house in ways they would never have thought of before. Even when I am in another part of the grounds, I feel that my privacy has been invaded.

Eventually the gate is replaced but this is by a modern cast-iron structure, hideously inappropriate, with its curli-cues and crosspieces. It doesn't offer any real security. And what is more, when it is shut, instead of a neat click there is a metallic clang. I only go in the garden now to mow the lawn or dig the vegetable patch. People-watching becomes an activity exclusively to be practised behind net curtains.

The Scourge of School

For the only child, school poses a threat to their security. Its relentless socialising is bewildering, even frightening. They are not labelled, but their characteristics often lead to their being singled out by their fellows and by their teachers.

This can lead to friendships being formed, especially with other Onlies, or with teachers who are sympathetic to their predicament.

It can also precipitate bullying on an alarming scale, by other pupils in the playground, and in the classroom by teachers exercising their powers in unacceptable ways.

Adjustment between home and school can cause problems, and may result in exhaustion and depression. Where a boarding school is involved, no relief from subjection to social norms can prove intolerable.

Picked On

He is no much bigger than me but he has a larger mouth. He has a more limited vocabulary but he uses it to greater effect. His name is Buller and it suits him. He comes from a family of six and they live on a council estate.

'Come here, pansy boy!' he yells. 'Turn out your pockets!' He cuffs me.

'I don't think I've anything here you might want,' I stammer.

'Well we'll soon see about that.' As a preliminary, he tears the badge from my blazer and tosses it across the yard. He rummages in my inside pocket. 'A pen. I'll have that. I can sell it.'

'My granny gave it to me.'

'Thanks, gran.' It has gone into his satchel already.

'Now listen here, you soft-arsed little runt. Tomorrow you bring me something from home I can really make money on, understand?' He hits me again.

'But that's stealing.'

He laughs and spits in my face. 'You'll do it, or else. You'll go home so black and blue mumsy won't recognise you!'

* * * * *

Days later Buller says, 'Come on, Killick, you're going to help me with this. Let's get that toad Chalmers in a corner and give him a duffing. You hold him down while I hit him. And then we'll see what he's got on him.'

Somehow I have managed to get in with him so that he considers me one of his gang.

Three Teachers

School is private and local and deeply dysfunctional. The head (and proprietor) is a man of violent mood swings. Every day he frightens me. When we arrive in the morning all the talk is of how he will be, of who will escape his wrath. On a good day he is laughing, chatting with the pupils, and blowing smoke in the faces of his favourites. On a bad day he growls at everyone and clips the ear of whoever gets in his path. Latin is indoctrination hour and English a little black book called 'Analysis'. In answering his questions he ridicules anyone with a trace of a local accent. One day his psychopathic tendencies take hold: he transports everyone to a field and spends the afternoon chasing us round and round beating our behinds with tree-branches till they bleed.

He employs staff with similar sadistic tendencies. One is a really nasty piece of work: he has a tongue like an adder flickering around our ears. His most spectacular punishment is to upend you in a waste-paper basket and hold you down till you cry for mercy. His sarcasm is particularly hard to bear from such a defenceless position. He is sacked – not for his inhumanity, but he commits the unmentionable crime of revealing socialistic tendencies in attempting to get elected to the local council.

Another is given the boot for calling on parents, ostensibly to discuss their sons' progress but actually to attempt to tap them for a loan. He has an odious classroom habit of standing behind you at your desk while you wrestle with the sums he has set: if it is going well, his open palm caresses the back of your head – if badly, you are suddenly sent sprawling.

One day we get our own back. He suffers from chronic dyspepsia and is always rubbing his guts and erupting. I win an essay prize and am invited to the Mayor's Parlour to receive it. He is chosen to accompany me, but finds the social atmosphere uncongenial: in a palace revolution of the pancreas, he upsets his tea down his trousers. On the back-row we live off his shrieks for weeks.

Conflict

My father returns from the city on the train after a day's managerial exertions. He is exhausted. I can see him wiping his balding head with a handkerchief. He rubs his eyes continually; they are dark pits in his face. The strain of being social is shown by the number of times as an insurance executive the fire brigade has to be called to put out his waste-paper bin.

He talks baby-talk with my mother – 'Mumsy', he calls her. She indulges his every childish whim. She appears to enjoy seeing him regress; it confirms her in the exercise of her power to make him the most dependent man on earth. He puffs at his pipe, cuddles up to her and turns the radio on. I deeply dislike his shows of unmanliness, his pathetic juvenile patter, and express this by pointed remarks especially about this pipe which I refer to as his 'dummy'. He knocks it out angrily on the fender, making the dottle fly.

My parents discuss my future openly. He wants me, his rival, out of the way at boarding school. This is rationalised by his ambition that his son will have some status in the world. My mother resists his attempts to have me removed from her orbit. Her interest is in extending her sway, not having it diminished. 'Let the boy be,' she says, cradling me in her arms. 'He's mine, and I'm keeping him here with me.' So there is this tug-of-war, and it is one which my father wins, despite my mother being apparently the stronger. I am the one caught in between, I am the one who is broken.

A Place Apart

Lying in the school sanatorium extension in the dark of winter, with the fire in the grate and shadows flickering on the walls, with only one companion – we grow close in complicity, ourselves against the universe. We talk of everything, never thought about before by either of us, nor broached since; there is a freedom to articulate, a hunger to share, no fear of ridicule or offence. We play games of chance, devised and known, filling all that warm cocoon with the mind's curiosity and precocity.

Thus by circumstance and invention we wholly manage to shut out that place of prefects, servitude, inkpots, impossible expectations, masters in black gowns lunging with caustic barbs...

There is only ourselves and the almost graspable entities of friendship and privacy. We never want the nights to end and each time dawn creeps through the curtains, stretching our world into the semblance of normality, we moan for the loss of our intimacies, our timeless time shattered by the clockwatching of others. When breakfasts appear on trays we fall back into our separate selves... and resume our roles of being ill.

Interrogation

'And what,' says the Headmaster, looking down his long
clerical nose at me, 'made you run away?'

'I hate this place,' I tell him.

'What especially?'

The answers tumble out: 'Cleaning prefects' shoes, being
beaten for not cleaning them properly, being held down in
the lavatory or in the dorm at night while older boys interfere with me, marching up and down in battledress in the
heat and dropping my rifle, losing the ball when fielding at
cricket, being laughed at because I like reading and writing
poetry, the dirt and smell of the locker room where we keep
our food-boxes...'

He holds up his hand to stop me. 'All these are experiences which will help you to grow into a man,' he says.

'Most of all, I don't have any time to be myself.'

My greatest regret is that I didn't run away more than
twice.

Sex and Onlyness

Most adolescents experience stress over their first sexual encounters. Onlies tend to approach them with even greater trepidation.

They will have lacked the casual knowledge gained from mixing with siblings. They may reject opportunities through anxiety, seeing any invitation as a challenge to their integrity and identity.

Onanism and Onlyness go together, and this may be a syndrome it is difficult to break out of.

The first really passionate mutual attraction may prove overwhelming in its impact and result in a commensurate over-reaction when it is not sustained.

Behind the Net

In this room the net curtains form a screen by which everything in the outer world is intercepted, processed and rendered innocuous. Cars glide by, footsteps and voices are muffled. It is as if everything out there exists only as a silent film projected on a screen.

But a girl, Elizabeth, appears. I do not know any girls, there are none in my family or at school. I know her name from once hearing it called out. She seems to be a couple of years older than myself, and lives further down the street on the opposite side. For months I have watched her secretly, admired her dark hair, her slightly swarthy complexion, her burgeoning figure, her long shapely legs. Almost every journey she has made past I have logged mentally. I have peered through the minute holes in the net, sometimes parting it slightly in order to see more closely; sometimes my breath has clouded the pane. Often she is alone, going on errands for her mother, or on her way to and from school. Sometimes she is with a friend of about her own age, occasionally with her parents, or a much younger brother. The sight of her always has the same effect on me. I long for her in a way that is both new and exciting and almost uncontrollable. It seems guilt-making because of its intensity and secrecy. My whole body flushes with anticipation. I long to be with her and touch her and have her touch me. On the few occasions we have met in the street I have been so embarrassed that I could neither look at her nor speak to her. She has never given me the slightest reason to think that she is more than vaguely aware of my existence.

One day she passes down the street with her friend and they are laughing and throwing up their skirts in sexual display. The eroticism of this is almost more than I can bear. Today the brother is with them and they are scolding him. He taunts them and runs ahead. When they catch him they punish him by pulling down his trousers and pants and slapping his bare backside. They only play at chastising him and he is laughing too. But I want to be there in his place, I want to her to pull down *my* clothes, have *my* buttocks exposed, feel her hands on *my* flesh and I know I would be shouting, 'Go on. Liz, hit *me* instead, you can hurt *me* as much as you like!'

Aunt Mabel

She is not really an aunt but it is what I have come to call her. She is really my mother's best friend from way back. She lives in the Midlands and comes to stay often, is almost an extension of the family. Now I am living back home attending the local technical college, she interposes herself between me and my parents, becomes my closest companion.

Mabel is 70 and has been a widow for more than a decade. She craves companionship and is responsive to art and literature. She is a woman whose sensitivities and talents have remained largely undeveloped. Her whole bearing, her appealing large brown eyes, the confiding tone in her voice, the slant of her body when she addresses you all tell the same story: a need for appreciation and love. When we go on family car journeys, she sits in the front and I am behind her. I find my hand creeping round the back of her seat to offer her reassurance and perhaps something more?

She invites me to stay during the holidays from my attendance at the local technical college, and this receives the parental blessing. She knows I have had a troubled time and wants to help. There may also be an attraction on her side which she hopes may blossom. Once we are thrown together, I realise what a striking woman she is: swarthy-skinned, with immaculately groomed white hair; with a keen fashion sense and wearing alluring perfumes, she would be a catch for any man. When we arrive at her house, we just drop our cases and fall into each other's arms.

She makes up a bed for me but I never sleep in it. She is childless and her body has the shape and texture of a much younger woman. She enjoys my body in a way she says she never enjoyed her husband's. He had been reserved and had always had to be coaxed to make love to her. We let passion rule. My greatest regret is that, for whatever reason, I am never able to penetrate her.

We draw the blinds and lie in each other's arms whenever we feel like it. We talk endlessly about our lives and I read reams of poetry to her. We are both aware of this as a time set aside, with its unique qualities of identification with each other. Mabel is more, much more, than a Mrs Robinson in her attitude and actions.

A fortnight (the original plan) extends to a month, but then I have to return home and to college. The parting is painful for both of us. I write to her every day and speak with her from phoneboxes. One day she understandably but foolishly writes back. The letter is intercepted. I am shown the reply, in my mother's hand, which forbids Mabel from ever seeing or communicating with me again, and severs her own relationship at a stroke. The whole of the blame for what occurred is placed on her and her name is never again mentioned in our house.

Smoking with Susie

She lights a cigarette, leans across the table, says, 'Will you have one?' I don't smoke but take one just the same.

She is sensual, cat-like in her movements, intelligent, alert, with darting mischievous eyes.

We are sitting on stools. The house is empty apart from ourselves; there is nothing to subvert our concentration upon each other. We talk about many things – people we know (the gossip flies), books we have read, music we like, places we have visited.

Paintings by her children are pasted all around, bright daubs – with much of the intensity that is her predominant quality. 'Another hour and they'll be back,' she comments.

'That's about the time I'll have to catch my train.'

'Another fag then?'

I concur. I can't resist anything she suggests.

More intimate chat. About how we came to meet and when we can expect our next time together. The future seems to stretch out as a series of delicious assignations.

'How about a coffee? I'm forgetting to play the perfect host.'

'You seem to be making a pretty good job of it.'

She slips off the stool and fills the kettle.

'What would you say if I told you I thought I was falling in love with you?' I venture.

Over her shoulder, without looking round – 'I'd say "Piss off" and mean it!'

Dream: Skyscape with Figure

I lie in the grass looking up at the sky, which is blue, far away and covered with a filmy gauze. There is a heavy insubstantiality about it. I shade my eyes from the sun and transfer my gaze to the tree: the leaves are a translucent green and turn this way and that in the breeze. They glint golden round the edges as the rays catch them. The tree is tall and they seem a chill canopy, sharp-etched, overarching.

Then she comes between me and the sun. She is wearing a cotton dress, shimmering blue like the sky, fringed with white laciness, and green traces seem to dance acidly before my eyes. She resembles but does not merge with the background: poised and impersonally remote, yet palpably close and tremulous.

I shall draw down that coolness, that warmth, and make them mine.

Breakdown

A substantial minority of the population experience some form of mental illness some time in their lives. How much has Onlyness contributed to this?

There can be many reasons for temporary instability. Difficulties in establishing and maintaining relationships is one.

Another is making one's way in the world. The biggest test here is whether one's talents are acceptable to others, when one has had little opportunity to weigh them up in the family situation, and school has provided an artificial environment of extreme competitiveness.

The workplace often requires qualities of cooperation for which Onlies have had little preparation.

Trust is an issue. Onlies may have difficulty in accepting help as the feeling of being on your own in all situations is difficult to overcome.

Away Again

I decide to train to become a teacher. This will give me years away from home, allow me to further my interest in literature and maybe I will make some friends.

I make one friend. Joe is a serious-minded gruff-voiced Northerner, with a lantern-jaw and a clubfoot. He is heavily into psychoanalysis, self-taught and stubborn. Night after night we sit up till the small hours; he is interrogating me; I am stumbling around in my head trying to find answers:

> What right have you to life – you who have been cursed with all the bourgeois trappings?
> You suffer a pipe-smoking executive father, and a doting nursemaid mother, and no siblings' dilution.
> They administered on waking the potion to immunise you from humanity.
> The creative spirit by which you put such store is no more than affectation.
> Like the coffee you drink in copious quantities the world is filtered out.
> You have no right to life. You are a parasite.

I had been put together delicately like some vase that stood high on a shelf – one note and I'd shatter, or a slight vibration might tip-toe me to destruction. First Joe climbs to a great height, thinking perhaps to save me from a porcelain existence. But he drops me, I am eggshell thin, I splatter at his feet. He kneels on the floor examining texture, tessitura, fracture through his one-eyed glass, a filigree dissection. At no point does it ever occur to him to glue any of the shattered pieces back together.

Dream: Stop the Carousel!

'Take me away!' I shout, but the thump and thunder in my ears from this monstrous mechanical machine drowns out my voice. It isn't that I don't know where I'm going. I know all too well that this device will bring me back in minutes to where I started from. It isn't that I mind the people I'm travelling with. I know all too well that they are on the same journey, and share the same fate as myself: to be unable to seek release and relief until some unseen, unknown person pulls the switch.

And then I see him, the man I love and hate more than any other person in the world, and he's sharing the carousel with me. He's on the back of a prancing horse about a third of the way round the turntable from me. He can't see me, of course, but I have a clear view of him, as his whole body weaves and dives with the swell of the merry-go-round. He's dapper and self-confident as always, sitting very upright, with arms folded, as if this is a contest and the winner will be the one who is least affected by the clamour about him. How like him to pretend to be unmoved, aloof from his surroundings, never admitting fault or allowing himself to be deflected from his aim.

Now I am oblivious of the shrill song and pounding beat, of the excited shouts of those around me. My concentration is upon the back of his head, neatly trimmed with not a hair out of place, and I think of the number of times the face which I cannot see has turned to me and smilingly lowered my guard whilst his words have stabbed home. We are on this gyrating monster together and suddenly all I want is to throw him off. I rise from my seat, steadying myself by holding onto one of the poles. It isn't easy when you are travelling at this speed and the circular motion makes me feel dizzy. I try to move from horse to horse, but they are almost all occupied and there is nothing to grasp at, my hand slides from one of the manes, and I fall onto the whirling board. I see the ground spinning close through the slats, before I am thrown clear.

The Consultation

I am sitting in the backroom of a doctor's surgery in my home town, drinking whisky with him.

'Feeling any better?' he asks.

'I could ask the same of you.'

'Well yes, now I've got some of this stuff inside me. I can't remember that much of today. One damn patient after another.'

'I can remember everything about today, every sharp detail, each piercing emotion. I'm keeping a journal, you know?'

'Yes, I suppose it's the equivalent of my AA confessions. Last night I sweated the truth out of me.'

'Does it make you feel any better?'

'Oh yes, I am cutting down. I am making real efforts to manage with only the minimum stimulus.' He raises his glass in recognition. 'And you, does the writing help at all?'

'It's a life-line. I'm working my way through all the traumas. Then I can read them back and get some perspective.'

'It's easier for you. You don't have to hold down an important job in the process. That's the hardest part.'

'On the other hand, there's no relief from confronting yourself. Every morning I get up and it's like starting all over again. And the whole expanse of the day is before you, and there's no escape from yourself.'

'That's the only child for you. Whereas I'm thrown into the middle of an endless line of social encounters. I've got to keep my head. I can't afford to make mistakes. The only times I can relax and unburden myself is in these conversations with you.'

This is the man who has been fighting alcoholism for years. This is the man who is offering me mutual support. This is the man who, less than a year later, fails to turn up in time at my home, where my mother is enduring a serious asthmatic attack and inadvertently kills her.

Night at Llangunllo Halt

After the last diesel has parped its way past, there is an involuntary indrawing of air as the landscape catches its second, deeper breath. These two elements predominate: the dark and silence.

On a night like this, with stars and moon to illumine, it is not really black but the obscurity is consistent. In towns there are always streetlamps or lighted windows, and even the clouds glow with reflected brightness. In country districts also, roads are raked by headlamps. Here what is dark stays so, scorning the encroachment of the walker without a torch.

Lacking the daylight's daily guide to familiar contours, a man might go mad. But I came for sanity's sake, in eager submission to another clime, a different order: this dark stretches back further than racial memory. Likewise the stillness: there is something absolving, clarifying about the quiet – washed clean of the pollution of cities, the urban stain, purified even of moral taint, of acts and sufferances.

The night is a void, a vast emptiness, resounding negation of all that the day has spawned in sensual excess, out of which small sounds emerge – discrete, unique. You are inside the echoing cavern: a sheep coughs behind the hedge. A man laughs… in the next parish. A screech-owl is in elemental pursuit of a shrew.

And these events profoundly have powers to restore. More than trains halt at Llangunllo. Lives, too, at a crisis-point come to pause and take their measure.

Eddies of Nanuto
(Hiroshige)

For the artist it is all regimentation – the waves lined up for inspection, folding out of and into each other, are hard-edged, impressively solid (for this beast has been tamed, it can never cry havoc). The flecks of foam will float there forever, like the birds hanging motionless above.

For myself, I'm immediately in there, powering everything into motion; the sea engulfs me; I cower in the depths between first and second surges; the tops tower perilously over.

But I know where I want to be: up there on a crest, breathtakingly buoyed up and braced and free.

Teaching Saves!

There is something special about entering a classroom as the person responsible for what occurs in there; it is both empowering and humbling. Once the teacher has got over early anxieties, a sense of responsibility for young lives takes over and gives purpose to each day. There is also the sense of superior knowledge which tempers any inferiority one may feel in relation to one's colleagues. Maybe this is rather ignoble, but so long as it doesn't get out of hand it establishes the conditions in which the psyche can flourish.

The only drawbacks the teacher faces are challenges to their authority, usually from individual pupils, but occasionally from whole classes. These can be overcome by skill and experience and the support of those in authority. The other drawback is having to withstand the cynicism of some fellow-teachers in the staffroom, but this just has to be shrugged off.

Teaching offers a profession which is both personally challenging and absorbing and is useful to society. It brings into play survival skills and sensitivities that come from one's situation.

The Pupils

I want, when the children enter my classroom, to create about them a little world, a microcosm of the world outside in which they will find levity and seriousness, pathos, praise, disappointment, kindness and sternness; in which demands will be made upon them which they must meet, thus insecurity and security occur, and everything with intensity on the small scale. However, I want there to be a difference: that all (so far as human fallibility permits) are to be judged according to their needs, what should be expected of each one of them; so the rewards are there, and there too the knowledge that somebody cares.

The Girls

When I turn from the board to the class and survey the girls, I am often awed by thoughts of their futures and how they belong in other men's cares.

This is a time when women still depend so much upon marriage to solve the uncertainties of career and security.

Then I look at them in turn, each one so alert and individual. By conscious and constant empathy I have come to know them, their loves and hates, personal mannerisms, idiosyncrasies of taste. And I am afraid for them in the time to come: how they will fare for guidance and understanding and whether they will be cherished for their uniquenesses.

Sandra

Gentleness is the characteristic and a charming reticence of
the eye; even more the lips shapely but dry. Until that day
she forgot her shyness and remembered how to laugh. At
the same time she vouchsafed to us serious glimpses of how
the world seemed to her: never anywhere happy, she said,
and found to her surprise that is how others saw it too.
Only they do not wish that they were dead.

Her contemplated life as a nun, for the reason that
she says, that nothing else on this earth seems to satisfy,
bemused and disturbed us. Whilst the world's indifference is
hard, consider this no cause or excuse for withdrawal.

And it is not wholly true: some few do care, and she is
far too fragile, beautiful and honest for us to lose.

Jackson's Due

For many lesson-periods he was no trouble to me: either he didn't appear or he sat at the back of the class reading a comic.

Then one day things turned a bit threatening. Jackson made his way slowly but purposefully to the front of the class until he stood between me and the other children. He delivered his verdict: 'Killick, you're an idiot. And if you lay a finger on me I'll get my dad up here to beat you up.' Then, in a pregnant silence, he left the classroom, slamming the door behind him.

The class looked at me and I looked at them. Everyone knew what a visit from his father meant: thump first, then thump again if it had not had the desired effect. I was wondering whether to mark him present or absent, but I resumed the lesson without commenting on what had occurred.

Later I went to see the Headmaster but with little hope of being taken seriously – he was famously weak and unsupportive of his staff. 'It's your job to keep order in your classroom, not mine,' he said. 'I'm here to establish and maintain the ethos of the school as a whole.'

A week later Jackson caused quite a stir by throwing his desk through the window of my classroom without opening it first.

Today the Head has deigned to look in to see if everything is running to schedule under my aegis. Jackson notices his arrival and reacts immediately. He picks up the full inkpot from his desk, walks to the corner of the room where the Head is sheltering and throws it with full force in his face. At first the Head cannot see; I have to help him with blotting-paper and a hankie, and lead him out into the corridor. Five minutes later he is back with his Deputy, and they haul Jackson, kicking and screaming, away.

I cannot dislike Jackson. I rather respect him for the consistency of his rejection of authority. He is a product of his upbringing, as I am of mine. The very qualities which enable me to get on with most of the pupils in my class are scorned by him. He has no use for kindness and empathy. In the communal situation I can make little progress in relationship with him.

I never see the boy again. I learn that he has been expelled from this Secondary Modern School and sent to an Approved one.

Supply

Why is it that you can never get everyone's attention at once? One boy is turned to the window; he is writing in the condensation with a finger. I issue a rebuke but he takes no notice. It is my first day teaching this class.

At break-time, I am given the information too late: 'There is one Special Needs in 6B. You will recognise clearly who he is, adopting strange postures and not understanding orders. Do not draw attention to him in any way.'

In the afternoon, when I take them, he rests his head on his desk, watching me closely from an almost upside-down position; he never smiles or frowns, or participates in the lesson in any way.

At the end of the day I hear fast footsteps behind me. He catches me up and is almost out of breath: 'Sir, sir, I should like to say thank you for the lessons.' A slight inclination of the head and he is gone.

Dream: The Face

I am in an educational establishment and the Principal, Daniel, an extremely warm and sympathetic man, comes and sits with me in the classroom. He initiates a series of discussions. Then there is silence. I say: 'Writing is one of mankind's greatest creations. And then to think of it being turned into print – that's amazing too.' Somebody else says, 'What about art?' I say, 'Art is amazing too.' Someone else says, 'Art is easy.' Daniel says quizzically, 'Art is easy?'

Then he gets to his feet and walks up into a kind of pulpit with a high back to it. He puts on a white robe. He is talking to us but we are mesmerised by the situation: he appears like a high priest. Suddenly he says, 'Art is amazing,' and is no longer there. There is just the white surplice floating in the air. Someone asks, 'What happened?' 'He did the vanishing trick,' I answer.

At that moment a panel slides open behind the pulpit and Daniel reappears smiling. 'You've seen nothing yet,' he says. And then his face goes through a series of transformations. It is like a jelly wobbling into and out of other faces, or like a Francis Bacon painting on the move. You can see all his ancestors one by one passing through his features at immense speed. And this is accompanied by laughter from all the faces. The whole thing ends on a primal scream.

Service and Sympathy

Onlies have to understand that the outside world doesn't owe them a life. It doesn't owe them anything: they have to deserve recognition.

One way of finding out what is possible is to put yourself in situations which are unfamiliar and call upon reserves you may not have used before. Sometimes this leads to an access of positive qualities. Sometimes you meet a brick wall and just have to lick your wounds and move on. Either way you're on a learning curve.

Occasionally, you find yourself in a social situation where you meet up with people of a different social background and with alien mores. You have to practise adaptation and drop your barriers to let your sympathetic side have full rein. Onlies are beset with self-consciousness and the instinct to preserve their independence.

Being of Service

I have attached myself to a college which has a number of
unique features. It was founded in the 19th century as a
place of learning and companionship. It is open to all men.
It charges few fees or none. There are no entrance exami-
nations. Guidance is offered to anyone enrolling as to the
level at which they might gain the most benefit, but no pressure is exerted on taking that advice. The clientele is a mix-
ture of races, ages and backgrounds. The communal rooms
are places where friendships are made and issues debated
passionately but with a civilised decorum. It has playing
fields, even though it occupies an inner city location. It has
a plethora of clubs and societies, including scientific, ram-
bling, chess, radio and drama; it has a symphony orchestra
and a magazine (of which I am currently the editor). I teach
there two evenings a week, events of great fellowship and
conviviality.

The college has a special atmosphere. You can be sure
of a warm greeting as soon as you walk in. Conversations
are entered into without preambles. Sessions rarely end at
the door but spill out into the streets, especially the pubs of
the area.

A really combative issue is the admission of women.
It would help the finances of the place, obviously make it
more representative of the society outside, but would also
change its ambience for ever. The debate rages on.

Like other teachers and leaders of activities, I receive
no payment for anything I do there. That is also something
that is under discussion. The practice has decades of history

behind it. There are a number of teachers on the roll who are not up to scratch. Other enthusiasts make a special contribution. The many professional teachers who add this to their weekly load believe that this is where they can exercise their talents more freely and experimentally than in the conformist system that pays their salaries.

Another issue is maintaining the balance between those classes which are there for their own sake, and those leading to qualifications which enable career advancement.

The college has ideals, it has traditions and it has a rare kind of integrity. Above all, it commands lifelong loyalty. I have more affection for it than for any other institution I have come across.

Seeing the Light

I am filled with transformative zeal. I will be able to tick off 'Social Work' next on my list of projects. I am employed by a member of the Scottish aristocracy to establish a pioneering centre for a community: The Lamp.

I fail to see that the landed gentry only recognise their own; they want the light to shine but just for their chums. I am determinedly democratic: that means folk music and photography. I have an ambitious plan for rejuvenating village halls as hubs for local populations. Vision comes cheap, I find, but realisation is expensive.

Meetings occur with the management at which dissent rattles the teacups. How long can such divergent views exist alongside each other in such an organisation? I have my supporters, some socialists, all profoundly social in their orientation. The founder has her champions, county, from across the shires.

On the day I am sacked I hand in my notice a few hours earlier, and make the front page of the local paper first.

What have I learned from this debacle? To read the runes, as well as the small print in a contract. And that the only light possible comes not from a beacon but a candle, which is lit with difficulty and easily snuffed out.

Learning to Love

There is a group of paintings by the Cookham artist Stanley Spencer in which he depicts couples who, to the spectator, seem to encompass extremes of ugliness; they are people from whom one would instinctively turn away. And yet these characters are revealed in poses of affection, even desire. One is in no doubt that relationship in two senses is being depicted: that between the couples, and that between the artist and his creations. These pictures embody love and constitute a remarkable but unremarked achievement.

There is a bus-station cafeteria in one of our large Northern cities which I pass through regularly. It is a working-class environment. Poverty and ill-health are predominant characteristics of those to be found here. The elderly are in the majority.

The place is an anthology of imperfection. In physical terms every grossness is on display. The unwashed are in evidence and some customers smell. The blind, the deaf and the otherwise handicapped seem to be in higher proportion here than elsewhere. More suffer from a palsy or have developed uncontrollable movements such as shuffling or gesticulating wildly. Voices conform to the same pattern: some people shout or laugh with excessive loudness, others mumble and fail to communicate their needs. Staff are patient and sympathetic but sometimes appear to totally misinterpret the ambiguous evidence presented to their eyes and ears. Occasionally they let slip an understandable irritation with the traits of a customer: as with the woman with a baby in a pushchair whose control of her offspring is less than ideal, and who usually allows the child to throw clean cutlery all over the floor and propel the pushchair down the steps in the café with a series of crashes; all this whilst paying the bill.

It is a place of low prices and rudimentary fare, both characteristics appreciated by the clientele. Some cannot wait to get to the table before they consume what they have bought. I have seen people refuse a plate and stuff the toasted teacake straight into their mouth. Others are so unsteady that they slop their drinks over counter and floor. One old lady refusing a saucer regularly loses the whole of the contents of her mug before reaching her seat and returns for a refill, with the likelihood of repeating the process. The rules of hygiene are frequently ignored. Food which is dropped on the floor is quickly shovelled back on the plate. Another old lady using a zimmer frame carries the change from her purchases in her mouth, spitting it into her hand when she reaches the counter.

Many of the faces appear time and time again: it is almost like a down-at-heel social club. The atmosphere of friendliness is palpable. Conversations between complete strangers are struck up and pursued with animation. There is an air of complicity – a 'we're all in this together' spirit prevails. Most customers want to talk once seated at a table, if only to themselves. I have overheard a number of meaningful monologues, and been subjected to some memorable harangues. The man who sits down opposite to me and without introduction unburdens himself of his erotic fears and fantasies does not seem out of place.

With so many imperfectly functioning bodies one is strongly aware of the physical. But ugliness doesn't come into it. If you regard these people as individuals in whom individuality is uppermost, then the dramatic differences from person to person become a series of manifestation of character. Condemnation or repugnance are thus rendered irrelevant. Rather, one rejoices at the astonishing variety expressed within the narrow frame of human possibility.

Music's Messages

Of all the arts, the one that speaks most meaningfully and memorably is music. Why should this be? Compared with words it has a greater immediacy of impact. Because it exists in time it can develop, make patterns, then repeat or change them, convey one mood or emotion, or several, suggesting stories or journeys without too great a specificity. However wide the span, it never loses its sense of newness.

In its classical essence there is a tendency for music to become too much set in stone, striving to attain a perfection of form and of performance which lacks spontaneity. Jazz has stepped in to provide that missing improvisatory element.

Onlyness finds its ideal identification in some music. It also provides instances of integration of the self into larger wholes. Music provides paradigms of how we are and of how we could be. It is an essential exemplar.

A Musical Conversion

I hate classical music – it is middle-aged, stuffed-shirtish stuff. I'm into big bands. I especially like The Billy Cotton Band Show. I crane my ear to the radio, not just for the drum solos, but every slight tap sends me into ecstasies. I recognise this as down-to-earth, warts-and-all entertainment, and I want to be a part of it.

My father, on the other hand, is a classical buff. He loves choral music, particularly oratorios, most of all Elgar's. When I pass through the room and he is listening to one of his favourites I stamp about hurling insults with the kind of force only a son teetering on the edge of adolescence can muster. As the days and months go by, my contempt intensifies.

Then one day, on my way upstairs to my own listening enclave I am stopped short by what he is listening to. I ask him the title. 'Afternoon of a Faun,' he answers. I sit down. I am gripped by the sounds, powerless to leave the chair.

'Is there any more music like this?' I ask.

'You could try Delius's 'On Hearing the First Cuckoo in Spring',' he suggests.

He has it in his record collection. I listen. It has the same mesmerising effect. I realise that, as with the big band music I am addicted to, it emanates from a group of musicians. But its effect is entirely different: it comes from one individual and speaks to the aloneness that I feel. I play 'The First Cuckoo' till scratchiness undermines its sense of allure.

It is time to move on. So far these pieces express a single mood, one of peacefulness and an identification with nature. Are there other moods to explore? It is only then that I perceive that, like the novels I read, such music can express a pattern of feelings, sometimes resolved, sometimes left hanging in the air. I am about to learn this lesson in a most dramatic way.

I hear a short, strident piece lasting less than five minutes which builds to a piercing climax then falls away again. It is fierce and urgent and yet in complete control of itself. It is an orchestral prelude by Shostakovich. I go to the local record shop and ask for the composer.

'I only have the Sixth Symphony.'

'Well I'll have that one.'

I discover that this piece nearly an hour long is spread across a number of shellac discs. And I only have sufficient pocket money to buy one.

'But I must have it!' I wail.

The shopkeeper takes pity on me: he sells me the first record, whilst putting the others aside for when I can afford them.

Thus it is that I listen to that part of the long first movement of this work up to the point of its massive climax. And I listen to this over and over again, totally frustrated by not hearing what comes next. Each week the musical plot becomes a little clearer. I find out so much about structure and contrast from this one extended listening experience. I am learning to love Dmitri by instalments.

Dream: The Concert

The music blares. Why amidst all this silence is music coming through that door? I knock. No answer. Nobody can hear me above all that din. Very gingerly I edge open the door, to reveal a large studio with an orchestra and conductor. The music is some cacophonous modern score full of bumps and rattles and outbursts of seemingly disorganised sound. Microphones hanging from the ceiling suggest that a recording is taking place. I can see a control room up at the back.

I fling the door wide and stand there with my hands over my ears. It is all too much. 'STOP!' I yell. The discordance dies away. Every face in the hall is turned to look at me. I feel small, guilty, frightened. A cultured voice replies, 'Yes?'

'I just wanted to know what is going on,' I say, in as insignificant a way as possible.

'Do you want us to go on playing?'

'I don't know.'

'Well this is your concert, you know.'

'I didn't. I don't like this piece,'

'You are free to choose something else.'

'I don't know what to ask for.'

'The programme is yours.'

'I think I prefer silence.'

'That is your prerogative.' The conductor lays down his baton. 'We remain here at your command if you should make a different choice.'

I surprise myself by what I do next. I shout, 'I REQUIRE ABSOLUTE SILENCE NOW!'

I am embarrassed at my vehemence. Everyone freezes in the position they are in at the moment I utter my command.

Now I feel strong, powerful. 'Good. That's just as I like it. Nobody make a sound. Nobody move a muscle. I'm going for a walk.'

The moment I close the door the music blares again.

Tallinn '97

First the strings hint at tragedy to come, a life style settled, self-sufficient, circumspect, over which will tramp deliberate, destructive squadrons of well-drilled boots, leaving woodwind desolation in their wake.

Then the composer grabs fistfuls of military brass and shakes the sheer audacity out of them in the scorn of his scherzo's horns.

Comes a calm in which he shows how it might have been, could be again, till we are plunged back into war's alarms. There is no escape for the citizen as the state machine rolls relentlessly on. This peroration is no triumph – no glorification of the Revolution, no recantation of aesthetic wrongs – as hollow as the timpanist's drums.

Three years on (after the troops have moved out), everyone in this concert hall understands the drama that has unfolded. Hardly a family free of the touch on the shoulder striking terror into the heart of the community.

Everyone merits a flower to take home to a loved one, as seems the custom in this country.

Improvisation

When I listen to Jessica playing solo, Onlyness is energised:

> 'I made it up to Rachmaninoff then discovered jazz.'

What she discovered was: plangencies and angularities, wry harmonics, stride and slide, cascades, staccatos, distortions and contortions, jokes, sly pokes, kaleidoscopes:

> 'I was four years old and I pressed a note and I saw an orange ball of colour, and since it was orange I think it was either D or F, one of those two notes.'

Synaesthetic chordings, swinging stompings, whole-tone happenings, journeys without a known destination:

> 'When you play jazz it's like walking through a forest. You stop and look at the trees and the moss and the little critters, and it's like everything's new, and every path you go goes somewhere else, and you find new wonder.'

Imitations and absorptions:

> 'Erroll Garner, McCoy Tyner, Ray Bryant, Kenny Barron – all the great inventors.'

Monkish melodies:

'When I first heard Monk I thought "God has got his boxing gloves on".'

Endless attempts to colonise the moment:

'Now is like a small gnat that you'll never be swift enough to swat.'

Unfolding identity:

'Music brings me self-knowledge I wouldn't get in any other way. The only person I can be is Jessica Williams, and I can be that only if I let myself go. I'm only as much musician as I need to be to let the music play unimpeded.'

Leoš and Me

I can't be sure which music of his I heard first; it must have been over 50 years ago. Perhaps it was the brazen 'Sinfonietta', one of the incandescent string quartets, or the achingly nostalgic 'In the Mists', but I know I was hooked.

Photos show Janáček to be an unprepossessingly-featured little man, a grocer or a tax collector, not immediately striking in any way. So what is it about the sounds he created which so captures my imagination?

Well he undoubtedly had a great soul, an uncommon capacity to empathise with the condition of being human in a variety of situations, and to express solidarity through melodies that are palpable and genuine.

He was close to ordinary people and their music making, and he made large-scale statements through them rather than about them.

He absorbed their folk-idioms, noted down their turns of phrase and of voice, and turned them into motifs. He orchestrated their soliloquies, their declarations, their hesitations and despairs. He fashioned their strengths and weaknesses into dramas that raise you up and cast you down.

Unrequited love is an emotion that came to dominate his life. He was in a loveless marriage, and adored a younger married woman he first saw when he was 63. From that moment he poured his passion for her, directly or sublimated, into everything he wrote.

Leoš's music turns the personal into the universal, the small into the overwhelming. This intensity and immediacy is perfectly captured in his diary entries:

> The tame look of a duckling, or the scanning glance of a hawk; an ardent kiss or the grasp of a cooling hand; the misty blue of the forget-me-not, or the burning fire of a poppy: all these create in me a chord.

Música Callada
(after Mompou)

The music begins. It does not tell you where you have been. It does not tell you where you are going. It holds you in the immediate moment but informed by an awareness of both past and future.

It inhabits a fragile no-man's land, walking a gossamer thread of possibility. It is always ambiguous. It exists on the threshold of audibility. It is composed of echoes and premonitions.

No journeys are undertaken, though you do not end where you began. You can take nothing with you but the essence of self. There are no companions: Onlyness is sufficient.

This is your time for meditation without words. You will not know when the music ends and the silence begins.

The Power of Words

From an early age, the words dance before you. You have a choice: either you shut them out or you dance with them. They have the capacity to enchant, to inform, to bewilder, to enhance. Once you are in their spell they will never let you go. No lifetime can be long enough to exhaust their possibilities. But reading them may not be enough.

You can save your life through the words. The simple (though oh so complex!) act of putting them down on a page somehow has the capacity to make clear what before was puzzling. Sometimes it makes you realise how intimately interrelated things are. Sometimes it takes you completely by surprise and thoughts and feelings emerge you never knew you had.

Words keep you in touch with the inner life. At times when you are in danger of losing that connection they restore it – that is their salutary power of salvation.

Literature Like Life

This is a poem by Stanley Cook:

View

Here in the North, often at the end
Of an uphill road the houses open out
To a view, like finding a hole in the roof.
Some attic or chimneypot is silhouetted
Marking the final foothold on the sky.
The wind combs out grey tugs of cloud
And as the threatened snow descends,
Blanking the view, sometimes you hear yourself
Resume for a word or two the conversation
That ended unhappily years ago
And whose unhappiness you know you had better
bear.

These 11 lines, as well as describing an urbanscape, present a complete outlook on life. It is an intensely sad one. Every detail contributes to that impression: the road goes 'uphill'; the view alarms 'like finding a hole in the roof'; a blizzard cuts off your vision; and the last straw is the uncovering of a grief which seems prevailing and inescapable – the final and longest line seems weighed down with it. The grief is undefined, and we can all supply our own. Others of Cook's poems express a humour and a jauntiness, but this one encapsulates a tragic quality which is universal. There are times when I can fully identify with it.

I knew and published Stanley, and loved the man. One day I was driving him from Sheffield, where he lived, to Halifax, where he was to give a reading, and we came to a short tunnel under the M62 that suddenly opens out into a panoramic vista of the Calder Valley. He remarked, 'This is my favourite view in the world.' In this he expressed his wonderful sense of social solidarity. He expanded on this in a poem about the scene, a much more positive view in this than in 'View':

> The hole is a peephole, much as a single life
> Must once have been on an age;
> You see it all and have to become a part.

Dream: A Visit From George

From my cottage window I see the bus draw up down the street and a workman-like balding man descend, carrying a capacious leather bag – is it full of tools or poems, I wonder? Answering the knock, 'George Barker from the Poetry Transmission Service,' he announces with a grin. I take him inside and make him comfortable in an armchair.

I offer him whisky. 'Not allowed to drink on the job.' This is a much more subdued George than I had anticipated.

'This is just the day job,' he confides. 'Only one day a week actually, but it helps to keep the proverbial predator off my threshold.' We talk poetry for a while. This, it seems, is permitted. I ask him why he excluded one of the funniest poems I know, 'Scottish Bards and an English Reviewer' – the one that ends with him making his way to 'a sottish bed and a Scottish day' after a night of carousing with the makars – out of his *Collected*. He seems evasive on this question.

'I have the poem here,' I say, taking 'The View from a Blind I' from the table.

'Sorry, can't do that. It's the ultimate transgression, for which I could be struck off. You're only allowed to listen to poems from your radio.'

'Well I can't hear them from mine. That's why I've called you in. Not exactly true, though, I can hear *some* poems.'

George is clearly intrigued. 'What exactly is the problem?'

'I can hear sonnets.'

'Odes?'

'No.'

'Villanelles?'

'Never heard one of those. Do you think the poetic thought-police are after me?'

'Doubtful. What about narrative poems – ballads for instance?'

'You must be joking. Would you care to take a look at it?'

'Sorry, not allowed to on this occasion. This is a purely diagnostic visit. Your radio is suffering from selective poetic amnesia. Perhaps I could call back again when I'm off duty?' asks George, eyeing the bottle of whisky.

Don Quixote Drowned

I have loved the work of the novelist James Hanley ever since in my late teens I discovered in the Tulloch Library a book of his with this title. Each year for more than a decade when I went up to the west of Scotland, I would take this book out and re-read it. It became a ritual to which I would look forward. I never tired of the narratives or of his way of telling them. I became particularly attached to the title story, where Crawley, the bullying sailor, forces the deckhand narrator to throw all his beloved books into the sea.

Since then I have collected most of Hanley's books, but not *Don Quixote Drowned*, perhaps because it was so clearly imprinted on my memory.

I suddenly had a strong desire, after all these years, to recapture the pleasure of holding the book in my hands again. I went online and found on Amazon just one copy; it was described as 'in very poor condition' and was extremely cheap, but I sent for it.

And now it has arrived. It is dog-eared and dirty, and I am opening it with trepidation. I need not have worried – the thrill is there from the opening words. Then something makes me turn back to the title page. To my astonishment I see the stamp 'Tulloch Library'!

To North

It's like gravity in reverse, this attraction to north. The needle swings, pointing you upwards towards the tip of the stalagmite, out of your comfort zone.

It keeps you alert, alive, no giving in to southern softness. It keeps you moving, planning, searching, exploring possibilities – you need all your energies just to keep going. And going beyond is sheer extravagance. If you've anything to spare, it must be held in reserve for even harder times.

It forces you inwards, exploiting solo resources. This is where the experience of Onlyness comes into its own. A concerted effort becomes especially meaningful in these circumstances.

Its hardness, its edge, provides the essential spike to create.

Anglezarke

As Edward Thomas his Adlestrop so I my Anglezarke, but with this difference: for him it was the name on the station sign and the tranced afternoon; for me now it is the name only – the rest clean gone – conjures the feeling, but there must have been more: water, woods, fields, for such a place to have become (as it has done) a touchstone for stilled security.

Strange how a 'sweet especial rural scene' can leave not even a trace on the slides of childhood. And yet what it *means* is with me for ever. Perhaps it has gone through rocks like rain in limestone country to form an underground stream of memory? Then this writing becomes the mind's potholing.

The Parental Pull

You can leave home, you can lose them through illness or disaster, or by choice and never seek reconciliation, but you can never escape them.

You have their DNA, you have unconsciously absorbed their outlook, their social attitudes. Your reaction to them can shape your life just as much as if you remained within their purview and protection. You will pass it on, somewhat diluted, to the next generation just as surely.

If Onlyness is part of your inheritance, for good or ill, they will loom larger than if others shared the burden and the opportunity. However much you struggle to throw them off, you will have to come to terms with them sooner or later.

My Late Father

When I think of him, this is the image which comes to mind: with my mother he is stitching a small tent of endearments from which, against her will but at his insistence, the flap is closed against me.

I can't ever imagine him in his work-role; I can only with difficulty imagine him apart from his wife, and their inimitable lapsing into baby talk and self-servitude.

We clashed over everything: music was the least of our battlegrounds; indeed I was to find myself in later years worshipping at the same shrine. A similar conflict occurred over literature: but with John Masefield and Charles Morgan no chastening conversion occurred.

After her early death, he never again tuned into concerts, or read words which strayed beyond the confines of newsprint. Golf-clubs and fishing-rods, well-meant retirement gifts, lay unused in corners of my Clydeside bungalow where he ended his days. He spent his time sleeping in front of a TV screen. There were no photographs to be seen: he had systematically destroyed every one in which my mother's image appeared.

He who never learned that we are judged by the standards we set ourselves, stayed shuttered, shut down. Mother-love transferred to a spouse, could not survive as consolation once the partner was gone. On my desk my final photograph of him: still physically present, but the light has drained from pursed-up eyes. Beside the picture, miniscule but meaningful, lies a pine-cone like a shrunken breast.

Searching for a Grave

I have not seen my mother's stone for more than 40 years, and now I have come humbly to read, acknowledge, receive, return love so freely given.

But how am I to find her grave? I scramble over tussocky ground, searching the faces for recognition. Some are prinked and house-proud; some fountain flowers at head and foot; some seem to have been grubbed up by rabbit or a passing rodent; some have fallen flat; some have even been beheaded (could it be in some family feud?); some have had their messages eroded by time and weather and neglect – is the one I am seeking one of those? Has it been broken and removed? What right have I to expect it will be waiting there for me to dispense consolation despite decades of disrespect?

Then, after almost an hour of 'In loving memory', 'Much missed' and 'Gone to a better place', I chance first sight of the name I crave. I kneel on the ground before the one stone that tells my story.

Dream: River

I am walking along the riverbank in a place I used to know well. It is a hot summer's day and the river is flashing as it travels over the stones.

The grass is springy to my tread.

Suddenly there they are – my mother and father sitting on a rug on the grass. There is a picnic laid out on the rug. They gesture for me to join them. It is a perfect place and a perfect time – how can I refuse?

I am a small boy again. I can feel the rough surface of the rug against my knees as I crawl onto it. My mother smiles one of her all-enfolding smiles and hands me a sandwich and a cup of tea. My father is at his most relaxed – in his shirt-sleeves; for once his tie is undone. My mother is humming a song that is a favourite of hers. My father indicates a dragonfly skimming the stream. Nothing disturbs us. A car passing over a bridge could be in another county.

The meal finished and the remains of it packed away in the picnic-basket, I lie in the middle of the rug staring up at the wisps of cloud suspended in the blue. Gently, very gently, my parents take the ends of the rug and roll me tightly in it. When I am completely enclosed they lift me off the ground and begin steadily to swing me round. Faster and faster I travel. I experience the exhilaration of flight whilst remaining protected within my warm wrapping. I am fully alive and alert in the world right down to my toes and fingertips. I am in darkness but I can clearly see through the material everything around me.

Gradually the motion lessens and I travel closer to the grass. Eventually I make contact with the ground again. The rug unrolls and I spill out. I am elated and unhurt. I am aware that no-one is now holding the rug. When I have picked myself up even the rug has vanished. Without a backward glance I resume my walk along the riverbank.

Onlyness and Ageing

Every life is a platitude because it is in essence a carbon copy of every other, unless it is cut short by some catastrophe.

But we have meddled with the natural span, stretching it further and further like a piece of elastic. So far it has not snapped. Surely it is not endlessly extendable?

At the same time as elongating the time line we have encouraged the stretching of family bonds. We are creating a society of isolates.

Those whose life time lot is Onlyness have the most experience of what it is to be lonely and to survive. It confers on them the privilege of knowing how to ameliorate the solitude of others.

A Shared Miracle

I am going to a nursing home in a city in the north of England, where I work with residents on their life stories, told in their own words. Today I talk with Lucy, aged 90, and Edith, aged 94. What these two women have in common, apart from their advanced age, is that they have both led active lives in the world, whilst practising their faiths with dedication. Both bear witness to the power of the miraculous. However, though they have lived in the same house for months, they are on different floors and have never met.

Lucy was born in the city and became one of the first qualified midwives there. Over the years she has delivered thousands of babies and this has given her an enduring sense of satisfaction:

> I can say that I was welcomed with open arms wherever I went. I retired officially in 1952. But I never really retired. I carried on, but I never stood in anyone else's light. Generations of families are grateful for the work that I have done, and this makes me feel very happy. Occasionally someone comes in and says, 'Nurse, you brought me into the world.' They don't let me forget, you see. But it is a long time since I performed these services. I have outlived the rest of my generation. There has never been a temptation to have children of my own. As far as men are concerned, my life has been filled with grateful husbands.

By contrast, Edith was born a German Jew in Upper Silesia. She had also devoted her life to service: she worked amongst the poor, helping working-class mothers to bring up their children. Unlike Lucy, Edith married: a German Protestant who worked as an architect for Hitler. This introduced many stresses into their lives, particularly after the birth of their two children and the rise of Nazism prior to the outbreak of the Second World War.

Edith was to have many dramatic experiences after her children were grown up and before finally settling in this country. She spent some years working in Africa. She had been attracted by the humanitarian ideals of the Quakers before experiencing their caring at first hand, and became a Friend when she was 66 years old. The last words in her life story read:

> Now I am 94, my one wish is to die: the desire to live leaves you when you do not have your health, and life for me has become such a struggle.

I tell Lucy and Edith about each other, and they want to meet. I arrange for this to happen on the eve of my next visit, at the very time actually that I am typing the final paragraph of Edith's story. I believe it was a memorable event: both recognising a strength – indeed, an indomitability – in each other and a common adherence to spiritual values.

Edith dies early the following morning before I arrive at the home. When I go to see Lucy, she is radiant rather than downcast:

> We met and talked, and it was in every way a special occasion. And then she was content to die: I regard this as a shared miracle.

A Challenge

'I wonder if you could do writing with people with dementia?' muses a company executive.

This is 1992. I have heard of dementia. I know nothing about it – it is hardly mentioned in the media. I have never met anyone with the condition. I say, 'Ok, I'll give it a try.'

This is how I come to be in an old, sprawling care home in the North Yorkshire countryside, where there are 80 residents, all with the diagnosis. The manager is dismissive: 'Complete waste of time sending you here,' he says. 'Do you know what you're letting yourself in for?'

'I think I should at least find out what is possible,' I venture.

'Well you must be as mad as they are!' He takes me to the door of a unit which he unlocks. 'There are 30 people with Alzheimer's in there. You won't get anything out of any of them.' He pushes me through and locks the door behind me.

Glimpses

I am flying over continents. Looking down, I can see that the clouds form three distinct layers. None of these, though, completely cover the portion of sky they occupy. There are breaks in the uppermost of them, permitting glimpses of the middle layer. Similarly, there are breaks in that layer which allow for flashes of the lowest layer. There are three sets of inconsistencies, and it is rare for them to coincide. Where this does occur, snapshots of the land beneath appear. It is a shapeshifting scene, continually thwarting the traveller who attempts to gain perspective as the plane speeds on.

It may be like this for the person with dementia, experiencing confusion with sporadic moments of clarity. It is certainly like this for those who would communicate with them: intermittent instances of illumination occur, and for a short while we are able to see the person as they are, coherent and whole.

A Sufficiency

In the photograph, we are standing in the unit, my left hand clasping hers. I, being much taller, am leaning forward, our heads are almost touching. We are laughing; Mary's eyes are closed, with the intensity of the feeling, it seems. It is a shared joke, but since she has little language left it may be something we have seen and identified. Or it may be that one of us has thought of something and the merriment has spilled over onto the other. As always there is a complicity that goes beyond words.

Bodies play a big part in our relationship: we hold and hug and kiss. We are always on the move – dancing or walking – exploring our environment. She never seems to tire of new places and faces; or rather the old places and faces seem to her ever-new.

Photographs are amongst her favourite things. Her face mirrors the feelings they evoke in her, and she keeps up an appropriate commentary. I can tell that by the tone of her sounds. Her discourse is full of exclamations.

Mary's gestures are full of exclamations: when I come on the unit and she sees me in the distance she approaches, always pointing, pointing. And I do the same. Until our hands meet and intertwine. She keeps saying 'Oh you!' over and over, as if she cannot believe her good fortune. I cannot believe mine.

She talks to mirrors. I creep up behind to try to find out whose image she is conversing with; each time she catches sight of me and turns round. But once I manage to get close enough to hear her sister's name.

When she has a birthday celebration with her daughter and her husband, she refuses to sit down at the table until I join her to help blow out the candles on her cake. Writing this, I realise I hardly know anything about her past life. What we have is all in the here and now. It is enough.

Ian and Me-ness

'I hate poetry,' he says. 'I did plenty of that rubbish at school!'

I am in his house with equipment loaned by the BBC, the intention to record the process of making poems out of the words of people with dementia. He was not keen to take part but when I told him that all he had to agree to was chat for a few evenings and I would see what I could do with it, he readily indulged me.

I had met him a few months earlier at a conference when he had intrigued me by saying, 'When I saw you striding along in the distance I thought, "This is the man who will do the job for us." You are a mysterious comet that flies in and out of our universe.'

Now it is he that is doing the striding, about his living room while loudly emoting and occasionally kicking over the microphone in his enthusiasm:

> My attitude is: there's just like a halo or something
> and it has to be there. Because that's the kingpin,
> that's the bit that sees up, down, over – all these
> things, and that's the thing you really have to take
> care of, otherwise you can get hurt very badly and
> very quickly.

I can make poetry from this and there is much more from where this comes from.

When I read his poem back to him he says, 'Those are not my words. I didn't say any of that.' I play him the tape and he's convinced: 'My god, I'm a bloody poet!'

After the last session, I ask Ian what he thinks of poetry now:

Essence of essences. It's what goes in and comes out. What matters to me is the me-ness of it.

Approaching the Mystery

She lies in a wide armchair, back to the window, with the sun streaming through the glass. It is being used as a kind of bed. She is supported by pillows, with her body wrapped in a blanket and a teddy bear laid to one side. She seems very old, and her face is hollowed, lined and pale. Her hair is white, thinly layered and straggles down her cheeks. The glasses perched on her nose seem like an afterthought. The lounge of the nursing home is hers alone, apart from my presence as a visitor. The room is without sound.

One can tell she is alive by the measured rise and fall of her breast. This, one feels, is what essentially her life has come to: the steady intake and exhalation, a heartbeat, a pulse – the mechanics of existence.

How could it be otherwise? Probably speech has gone and medication makes sleep the only option. Choices have been winnowed to this last alternative – to breathe or not to breathe? Which is no choice at all, since she is unlikely any longer to have the capacity to exercise it.

So how much of the human remains? Is what I observe the last unwindings of a spring set in motion by her conception, wholly predictable in its trajectory? Does she still dream? If dreaming requires the experiences of everyday to feed it, then maybe the stream of unconscious processing has dried up? Or are her fantasies still succoured by a lifetime's memories? The body's dissolution may have robbed her of mobility and her mind's capacity to observe and process in a conventional way, but 90 years of bombardment of the senses, engagement of the emotions and interpretations of reality must surely be still there, miraculously preserved, but inaccessible to others? Whatever social life she may have led, she has largely returned to Onlyness.

The ends of our existence dissolve into pure mystery. This lends a sense of challenge to them. Without travelling out from and towards the unknown we might be tempted to lapse into the kind of mindless habituation which can beset our middle years. It keeps us on our toes intellectually, sharpens our spiritual reflexes. Why were we given consciousness of self if not to ponder the possible obliteration or enhancement of the spirit?

Throughout these reflections, the woman on the chair in front of me does not appear to have moved. She has vouchsafed no clue as to her awareness of her situation. She remains half in bed, half out of it; perhaps half in life, half out of it. My empathy goes out to her in her profound isolation... do I imagine a slight pressure of her hand in response to mine?

The Barrier

I am standing in front of a door I cannot open. My hand goes out and clasps only empty air. Over and over I will myself to grasp the handle, but to no effect. I am bewildered and distressed. The tears fall down.

Inside the care home, there are appointments to keep, people to see, words to hear and transcribe. But it is no use. Eventually, after long minutes I turn and walk to my car.

* * * * *

Back home, I ring my friend, a psychologist, and describe what happened. 'You must seek help,' she says, 'but not from me. You will have to see a counsellor.'

I pour out my story to a stranger: how I have discovered this special talent for relating to people who lack communication, empathy. And now by not delivering it I am letting them down. 'I can't go on,' I say. 'I'm having a breakdown.'

She replies, 'You have emotional overload. Week after week you have taken upon yourself the griefs of others without addressing any of them. It is more than one person should expect themselves to bear. But the situation is remediable. And there is a positive way of looking at it: you have been changed by the experience. You are not suffering a breakdown – you are experiencing a breakthrough.'

Suddenly the barrier is raised and I can pass through.

The Point

Anatomy lesson: the pointer slithers down, patting each in turn: cerebellum, coccyx, ventricles, testicles (causing spurts of sniggers), pausing on corpuscles.

From where I sit, the marks it makes on the wall-chart's surface go further, though: if you hit the real thing like that it too rebounds, but the difference is that with the human it hurts.

And for years that's as far as I would – could – have gone. Then the frightened face pressed to the bars, the man with the gangling grin, the woman dribbling strange words down her blouse all day, hove into view.

And all is changed: I see that the pointer has fallen from the teacher's hand; I no longer need a map of the body; I am touched, I am pierced *here* – I bleed, I cry!

Dream: Finding My Way

I've arrived at the station, as so often before, coming out
and needing to get to the school or college where I study or
teach. I know if I go left I'll soon find myself out of town and
end up in a field where the footpaths lead in diverse direc-
tions burying me in woods or tall cornfields; none of these
are helpful because I've walked them all before. Whereas if
I turn right I'll be swallowed up by suburban streets where
all the houses look the same and I often end up in a circus
or a cul-de-sac. I catch glimpses of the buildings I'm looking
for but they never seem any closer and there is no clear way
through to them.

On the few occasions when I have broken out of the
maze and entered the campus it has never been at a point
where I have needed to be. Usually I find myself at the central administrative block and in the polished impersonal
hallway where the principal and all the other senior figures
have their offices. I don't enter their rooms for fear of dis-
turbing their privacy.

Where are my colleagues and friends? Where are the
familiar rooms, personal and communal? There is never
anyone to ask. I never seem to learn from my previous
mis-turnings. The only thing I can recognise is an all too
familiar sense of abandonment.

Towards the End

You never know when you might reach it. It could be today, tomorrow, next week, next month, next year, a decade away.

What you do know about it is that you get there alone.

You are increasingly beset by the deaths of those of your generation, friends and relations. This increases your awareness without necessarily preparing you for your own.

You tend to hang onto the moments for fear of the opportunity to fill them slipping away. You are increasingly conscious that you have spent a lifetime absorbing knowledge, making relationships, developing ways of coping, perhaps shaping elements of a creative vision. All of this will be snuffed out in an instant.

No-one can be fully prepared to accept this state of affairs. But maybe the Onlies are more reconciled than those whose lives have been crowded by siblings and their extended families. They have always lived with the knowledge of their essential aloneness. It makes some sense for them to shed everything except the essential self.

Secret Psyche

I am at the funeral of someone I have counted my closest friend for over two decades. He has died of cancer which has developed with remarkable speed. Either that, or for a long time he kept the information to himself.

A wisecracking Cockney with a sensitive side, short, thickset, with a square jaw, close-cropped white hair and twinkling blue eyes, Don was at least 20 years my senior. We met when I was running a creative writing class at an adult education college in London. He entered that first session hesitantly – he hadn't attended an evening class since he left school without qualifications and was doubtful if he'd be able to cope. He needn't have worried – his essays were feisty, highly opinionated, apolitical and atheistical; he was immediately popular and, most importantly, hit it off with the tutor! Most of us went to the pub afterwards and, on almost every subsequent occasion over the succeeding six terms, there he was in his element.

In the following years we both moved north and met frequently – over meals, at concerts, on walks in the country and holidays. Always the conversations scintillated, the confessions were freely exchanged.

Now I am listening closely as a young cleric begins his eulogy. How much does he know of my friend that is pertinent? Has Don at the end found God? He tells us that in recent months he has been let into Don's private thoughts and feelings. In particular he has shared his Second World War experiences (I always found this subject a no-go area both in speech and writing). I learn that he fought in Holland

and that he gained the highest honour for bravery that the Dutch government could confer.

I don't believe Don ever had a romantic attachment and I'm sure I was his closest confidante in the latter part of his life so it is unlikely that he ever spoke of these things before, until the proximity of his dying persuaded him to open up to a relative stranger.

How much do we really know each other? Is there a secret core in each psyche that we guard against intrusion, even from those who most have our wellbeing at heart?

I am brought up against the blank wall of my friend's separate selfhood, and sent spinning back into a realisation of my own Onlyness.

A Burial

Five burly black-suited men carry a box with my friend inside, then retreat in military formation.

She who was a wordsmith extraordinary, sensitive to wild nature and human foibles, brimming with sharp observations and contentious opinions, now lies silent in a container.

There is a silence too in this tiny church, with its overflowing congregation. A sudden bellow from behind signifies the start of a ritual. The voice is harsh and hollow. Its perpetrator passes through us rasping words of welcome, then turns in the pulpit to face us. Swarthy, with long black locks, askew gestures, restless eyes; his speech is out of sync, with emphases oddly placed, but he exercises an awful fascination, as he renders absurd the prescribed liturgical pronouncements.

Now he is attempting a celebration of one who was gentle, soft-voiced and an unbeliever; one who saw the countryside scrubbed of the sentimental patina of the past; one who strove to assert her own creativity in the face of the dominance of a famous and demanding husband.

But what is this priest proclaiming? 'I see two eggs in a nest. And now the shells have cracked and their bodies are being carried aloft by two white-winged angels.' I almost protest at this parody of a relationship.

And now I see my friend in her box being shouldered by the big burly men out into the churchyard. And now I hear the air at the graveside being rent by a gravelly groaning in which the only comprehensible words are 'dust', 'ashes' and 'amen'.

A crowd of crows rises cawing into the sky and a flock of sheep scatters from under a wall's shelter.

My Secret Valley

I travel on this line regularly to Scotland. It skirts the Lake District but I rarely look out, preferring to read or write or sleep. But today is different. The train has stopped unexpectedly and another passenger turns and exclaims, 'Look, what an amazing place!' I follow his gaze and there it is, my secret valley, fairly indistinct in the heat-haze, but I cannot mistake the contours. Despite plate-glass and distance, it is a fertile and fulfilling image.

In my childhood I often saw it. We would be travelling by car, before the motorway, before the concentration on speed and arrival. My father drove in a leisurely fashion, reflectively, giving plenty of time for looking. I would call out when it first came into view and sometimes he would stop, ostensibly for me to stretch my legs but I would be free to gaze. I tried to photograph it on my retina. I never once ventured into the valley – somehow my presence might interfere with its beauty.

It is a perfect U-shape, with a stream running through the middle and steep but not perilous slopes. There are occasional farms and many sheep dotted about, as if placed there purely to enhance the composition. The grass is intensely green but there is a blue haze in the distance. It is framed by mountain peaks.

Over the decades, I have kept that pastoral landscape in mind. Paintings of similar scenes have stirred the memory, or the hearing of a piece of music like Duke Ellington's 'Warm Valley' has conjured it up. More than once it has offered me the assurance that Onlyness need not be sad. It is *my* place, as RS Thomas puts it, 'somewhere to wear against the heart in the long cold'.

Dream: Last Laugh

I am shown into the room by an unctuous commission-aire-type man in a grey uniform with brass buttons and a peaked cap.

'Wait in here, please, sir.'

He shuts the door. In the centre of this small room, more a cubicle, are a table and a chair. There is no decoration of any kind to be seen, except that, incongruously hanging from the light-fitting in the centre immediately above the table, is a sprig of mistletoe. I walk round and round the table for perhaps three minutes, then the door opens and a dark-suited balding man enters; in his hand he holds a Christmas cracker.

'Sit down, sir,' he says, and places the cracker on the table. 'Your dinner is about to be served.' Almost on cue, the commissionaire returns with a plate of meat and vegetables which he places before me. Knife, fork and serviette are produced as if out of the air.

'Enjoy your meal,' says the Man in Charge.

As I pick at the turkey and stuffing, the sprouts and roast potatoes, he speaks to me, or rather someone who might be myself, as follows:

'The Last Supper is a repast with a long and auspicious, not to say sacred, history. Many have partaken of it before you, and many are destined to follow. These are moments to savour and digest. They say that in the last moments of a man's or a woman's life, the whole of that life will be replayed at lightning speed. You have 15 minutes at most in which to complete this task, whilst the inner person is satisfied...'

There is much more in this vein but by this time I have ceased to listen, being preoccupied with my own thoughts.

When I push away my plate, the Man in Charge says, 'There is sweet to follow: the traditional pudding with brandy sauce.'

I shake my head and stand up. As I tuck my chair back under the table I become aware once more of the mistletoe. 'What's that doing?'

'That's there for our lady clients. At this time of year some of them, perversely I believe, wish to avail themselves of a nostalgic embrace with a gentleman.'

'I suppose that means you,' I reply sharply.

He gives a practised chuckle. 'The male of the species in their turn are permitted of a penultimate joke,' he comments.

'And where does "the last laugh" come in?'

'Ah, that rests with Our Master and He, characteristically, has chosen to embody it in the form of that cracker you see before you.' He picks it up and proffers the other end. 'Please do me the honour of pulling it with me.'

As was no doubt intended, I succeed in being left with the larger half when the cracker splits. It is a no-nonsense affair, without hat or novelty. But there is a slip of paper which I unfold.

'There's not even a motto,' I complain. 'It's completely blank.'

A faint, world-weary smile flickers across his features. 'Exactly, sir. Now if you would please step this way...'

Creators and Inheritors

As composers, for me there would be – Haydn, Janáček, Mompou – but they have already gone into the Silence.

As artists, for me there would be – Turner, Hiroshige, Eardley – but they have all gone into the Darkness.

As poets, for me there would be – Wordsworth, Hardy, Edward Thomas – but they have all gone into the Blankness.

So was it worth it for them – the struggles with sounds, colours, words – all their talents obliterated by decease?

Yes, because the solitary acts of composition have become shared experiences in their absence. Like a continuous stream of sunlight, the rays of their inspirations have illuminated the lives of those who have come after.

They are the Creators; we are the Inheritors. We who, in however small a way, strive to emulate their endeavours, may in our turn hope to perish into communal consciousness.

Last Sounds

I want the sounds of tuning. First of all, the orchestra is one of mankind's greatest inventions, a conglomerate of kaleidoscopic potential, of endless possibilities of invention. It also symbolises (and actualises) what can be achieved through collaborative effort. I want to be reminded of that.

But I don't want the finished works, I want the sound-blocks out of which the musical architecture is constructed, the precursor of imaginative experience. That could prepare me for what is to follow. And if nothing is to follow, I shall go out to delicious expectation.

Check-Out

I am travelling solo. I set my hold-all down and unload its contents. Then I place everything, including the bag, on the moving rollers. These are the objects which disappear into the flaps:

A battered Dinky Toy double-decker bus, no driver in the cab, and two of its tiny tyres missing – perhaps part of a once-proud fleet?

a neat, maybe still useable board rubber, retaining traces of chalk around its soft stripey face – it exudes a primitive ignorance of the sins of omission it may once have committed;

lastly a splendid waistcoat, close-fitting, garish in its patterning of red hot pokers, a fashion accessory of a sort, a laughter-provoker for those facing end-of-life challenges.

I pass through the electronic portal unchallenged and stride away unencumbered, not casting even a glance behind me. The doors slide open and I step outside breathing in the endless air of afterwards.

Postscript

At its most basic, I guess reaction to these texts could be either 'Yes, that's happened to me too' or 'No, did that really happen to him?'

This has been one man's partial account of the experience of Onlyness. I am conscious of so much that has been left out of my story. The aspects I have chosen to emphasise may not be those someone in a similar situation might have chosen.

The relevance of individual entries might well be questioned. Some are there to fill out the picture of myself, my quirks and foibles. Some may appear more illuminating on later reflection.

I would like to think that, flawed though it may be, my little book can open up channels for consideration. The scattered nature of its structure seems appropriate for an account from a society where individualism is the norm.

Whether this work can be considered art is for others to judge. One of the questions I believe it raises is whether the condition contributes to inventiveness and creativity in the person and to what extent initiative is fostered or inhibited by lack of competition.

Leaving matters of quality aside, perhaps this work can be judged a crafty attempt to gain sympathy for Onlies?

Luath Press Limited

committed to publishing well written books worth reading

LUATH PRESS takes its name from Robert Burns, whose little collie
Luath (*Gael.*, swift or nimble) tripped up Jean Armour at a wedding
and gave him the chance to speak to the woman who was to be his wife
and the abiding love of his life. Burns called one of the 'Twa Dogs'
Luath after Cuchullin's hunting dog in Ossian's *Fingal.*
Luath Press was established in 1981 in the heart of
Burns country, and is now based a few steps up
the road from Burns' first lodgings on
Edinburgh's Royal Mile. Luath offers you
distinctive writing with a hint of
unexpected pleasures.
Most bookshops in the UK, the US, Canada,
Australia, New Zealand and parts of Europe,
either carry our books in stock or can order them
for you. To order direct from us, please send a £sterling
cheque, postal order, international money order or your
credit card details (number, address of cardholder and
expiry date) to us at the address below. Please add post
and packing as follows: UK – £1.00 per delivery address;
overseas surface mail – £2.50 per delivery address; overseas airmail –
£3.50 for the first book to each delivery address, plus £1.00 for each
additional book by airmail to the same address. If your order is a gift,
we will happily enclose your card or message at no extra charge.

Luath Press Limited
543/2 Castlehill
The Royal Mile
Edinburgh EH1 2ND
Scotland
Telephone: +44 (0)131 225 4326 (24 hours)
email: sales@luath. co.uk
Website: www. luath.co.uk